Assisi embroidery

Jos Hendriks

Hendriks en Hendriks
Vallière, Ostuni, Zeist
2017

Editors: Jos Hendriks, Luuk de Weert, Jos Hendriks
ISBN 978-90-821900-2-1
Copyright by Jos Hendriks
All rights reserved. Published by Hendriks en Hendriks

Design by Jos Hendriks

In memory of my wife Agnes Clijnk

Preface

It took about 10 years to make this book. Not that I worked the whole time on it. There were periods of months, even one period of more than 3 years that I did nothing. But there were also many 60 hour weeks that I spent creating the designs for this book. It is now the most extensive collection of important and interesting Assisi embroidery designs.

The designs are not meant to serve as a pattern for a piece of work that you make yourself, although. for most of the designs, it is possible to do so. And in that case, you will need to scan them, enlarge them and print them out. For the larger designs you will probably have to divide the pattern into several pieces before you can print them. In 2018 I will publish a second book with all the designs in this book enlarged and rasterized, making it possible to use them as a pattern. That book will be in black and white and thus not very expensive.

Every design took a lot of work because I had to draw every vertical, horizontal and diagonal line of the motives and fill in every cross-stitch and half cross-stitch separately. Furthermore, many designs are far bigger than the embroidery designs you see nowadays. All the works were created using the software package Coreldraw. That, of course, sped up the work and made it extremely precise.

During the last ten years I also created designs for embroidery with all the characteristics of Assisi embroidery except one. For example, I designed voided work with Chinese dragons as the motif. I decided not to include those, therefore all the designs in this book are purely Assisi. You can also find several "Chinese" patterns on my website (http:/www. stitchstitch.info) available for free. But not for long, unfortunately. It is sad that many sites on the internet that previously offered all kinds of information for free are disappearing. I also intend to stop with all the free stuff I offer because every pattern on my site has been stolen by the site Pinterest.

I hope you will enjoy this book. I know many of you buy embroidery pattern books with the intention of using one or more of the patterns, but sadly, it never happens and no embroidery work is made. But you never know...

With this book it is not so much of a problem because the designs in it are treasures in themselves.

December 2017

The author

Table cloth 160x160 cm, design 204, plate 70 and design 160, plate 39
Embroidered by Jos Hendriks

History

The embroidery style known as "Assisi embroidery" (in Italian "Punto Assisi") came into being around 1900.
One of the important characteristics of this style is that it is so-called "voided work". With this technique the motives are not embroidered but instead the background is filled in with embroidery stitches. There are quite a few preserved embroideries from the 15th, 16th and 17th centuries in which this technique was used. These embroideries include animals (real and imagined) and all sorts of recessed floral motives, just as the embroideries from Assisi and its surroundings after 1900 do. The Assisi works strongly resemble the older embroidery pieces of the 15th, 16th and 17th centuries. If nothing else, they certainly were/are used as a source of inspiration for the modern equivalents.

Italy? Spain? 16th or 17th century

We don't know exactly where these old embroideries were made. Most of the time only the country where it came from is known and sometimes not even that. Most of the pieces whose origin is known come from Italy, but there are also pieces that come from Spain, Portugal, and Greece. It is certainly not surprising that pieces in this technique were made all over southern Europe and probably also in parts of northern Europe. Ideas spread from place to place quite easily during the Middle Ages. And because the techniques used are simple, it is quite possible for a talented person to replicate it even after just one viewing. Moreover, after the Bible, pattern books were the first books to be printed. As a result, they spread all over Europe.

We know that voided work was made all over southern Europe. It is very possible that such work was also made in and/or near Assisi, but I cannot point out any definitive examples. Raffaella Bartolucci Cesaretti, in her book "Il punto Assisi, storia di un Ricamo Antico", without a doubt the most beautiful book about this style, also can't give examples. She devotes the largest part of her book to the period after 1900. From an earlier period, for instance, she notes a fresco of Simone Martini called "La vita di San Martino" which is in the basilica of Saint Franciscus. On this fresco you can see an altar cloth with motifs that are also used in Assisi embroidery after 1900. However, in that cloth, the technique of voided work is not used and the motifs present can be found in all kinds of embroidery all over Europe. It looks more like the designers from the first quarter of the 20th century were inspired by that fresco. There are also quite a few design examples made after 1900 that are directly based on reliefs found in churches in Assisi. There are also designs with motifs based on paintings on pews found in the cathedral of San Ruffino in Assisi.

The embroidery pattern from plate 44 (design 168) is completely based on this reliëf in the left side portal of the cathedral San Ruffino in Assisi

To me, the subtitle of Cesaretti's book is misleading. There is not an old style "Punto Assisi". There is no local tradition from which this embroidery work came into existence. Of course, the voided work technique is based on older work, but this technique was international. And the kind of motifs used (real animals, fantasy animals, floral motives, etc.) are also international and very widespread. Furthermore, the inspiration and examples for the motifs do not come from embroideries but rather from sculpture and decorative paintings. Also, there is no mention of "Punto Assisi" before 1900.

How is it possible that an embroidery style was created, more or less quite suddenly, in Assisi and its surroundings?

There is a good explanation. Around 1900, the industrial revolution turned European society upside down. Many people lost their jobs and were impoverished. As a result, and maybe also as a result of the emancipation movement of that period, an organizing movement started in Italy among women which tried to create opportunities to let them earn money. This happened not just in Assisi, but all over Italy. Women acquired the places and means to make lace or embroidery. Cloths, yarn and designs were all put at their disposal. More importantly, those organizations arranged expositions in Italy and abroad thereby creating selling possibilities.

In 1891, the "fra straniere" (between foreigners) society was established in Rome . The aim of this society was to introduce other countries to Italian lace, embroidery and cloths. They successfully sent work to the world exhibitions of Paris and Chicago.
In 1898 the different existing schools for decorative arts banded together under the motto "to support initiatives for the amelioration of the social, economic and moral conditions of women".

A share of "Le Industrie Femminili Italiane"

Of utmost importance was the founding on 22 May 1903 of the "Sociata cooperativa anonima per azione" under the name "Le industrie Femminilli Italiane". This was a kind of joint-stock company that issued shares that could be bought anonymously. The then king and queen of Italy bought a maximum number of shares. There was a committee of recommendation consisting of 25 influential Italians. The company was supported by the Banca Italiana, the Ministry of Agriculture, Commerce and Trade and by the administration of the city of Rome. The company had as its purpose "to revive the traditional techniques and arts in Italy and again to give dignity to the work of women." The words of Cesaro Vivanto during the foundation of the company shows clearly how that should be achieved: "We want to create a commercial instrument that opens international routes for all products made by Italian women. We want to create an enterprise that puts the intermediary trade which exploits our women out of action. We will search for a bigger market. We are going to combat bizarre, ugly and improper products. We will enlarge the revenues of women".

Subgroups were established all over Italy. Two in Umbria, one in Perugia and one in Assisi. As a result, there arose everywhere in Italy places where women could come together, where they could learn handicraft techniques, where they could get materials and designs and where they could sell their products for reasonable prices. Out of these places sprung new embroidery styles. You could certainly see that these styles were new, based sometimes on local tradition and sometimes not. That happened not just in Assisi but also in Bologna with the embroidery style "Ars Emilia", and in Casalguidi, a village in the municipality Serravalle Pistoiese, with the embroidery style known as "Casalguidi". There are many more examples but most of them were short-lived. For example, in Deruta, the style "Deruta2" came into existence. The embroidery in this style was completely different from what was made before in Deruta. Between 1910 and 1930, when this village had about 6000 inhabitants, a large part of the female population made Deruta embroidery. Then it disappeared. Now, as with other Italian embroidery styles from the first half of the twentieth century, it has been rediscovered.

Even today "Punto Assisi" embroidery is handmade in the town of Assisi and you can still buy it. Since 1900, Assisi embroidery has been made in Assisi. There are a few explanations for this. First of all, "Punto Assisi" is a style that gives relatively quick results and this makes it relatively cheap. And because Assisi is a tourist town, there are always possibilities to sell this work directly. Furthermore, there are several pattern books with good quality designs. This is the reason why there are also people outside of Assisi making "Punto Assisi" embroidery.

An execution by Jos Hendriks of a design on plate 67

Execution of the design 240, plate 90 by Jos Hendriks

About the style

Assisi embroidery is made from linen or cotton. The number of threads of the fabric, horizontal and vertical, has to be the same per centimeter. The embroidery thread that is used is most often cotton but it can also be silk. In Italy you can buy a linen fabric named Assisi ("tessuto Assisi"). This linen has 11 threads per centimeter and the fabric is 270 centimeters wide. This is enough to make a tablecloth for even the biggest table. Suppliers say that it is specially made for "Punto Assisi", but of course you can use it for other projects as well.

Assisi work is voided work. First the motifs are lined with the back stitch. In this lining none or just a few details inside the motif are outlined. Thereafter, the background is filled in with cross-stitches. Traditionally the stitches are worked over three threads of the fabric. The stitches are counted and every stitch has the same size. It is so-called countable embroidery.

Most of the time there is a decorative border around the work. There is the same such border on the up- and downside of borders with a repetitive design (Plate 11-designs 46, 48-49, Plate 12-designs 46-53), but also around medallions (Plate 16-designs 83-85) or around rectangular designs (Plate 56-design 185, Plate 71,72-designs 205 and 206).

Execution of a design on plate 63. There is a double decorative border

Assisi embroidery uses two colors which is different from older voided work which used just one color. One color is used to outline the motifs. This color is almost always black, but sometimes dark brown or dark green is used. The second color is used for the cross-stitches in the background. Most of the time it was red or blue but other bright colors that contrast with the first color can also be used. Most of the time the decorative border is the same color as the cross-stitches (Plate11, Plate12-designs 50-53). However, there are also many decorative borders that use the same color as that used in the outlining of the motifs (Plate 26-designs 124-125). There are also decorative borders where both colors are used (Plate 29-design 133, Plate 32-design 144). The decorative border is an essential part of the whole embroidery and can be doubled (Plate 34-designs 148, 150, 151).

Animals are often used as motifs - they are stylized and more or less realistic. Birds (swans, ducks, eagles and peacocks) are the most common, but you also find lions, deer, sea horses, fish and snakes. In many designs the animals are imaginary. Sometimes a known imaginary animal such as a griffon is used but it is not uncommon to see newly imagined species (Plate 30-design 135, Plate 32-design 143, Plate 38-design 159).

Then there are the floral motifs, often used to connect different parts of the design (Plate 53-design 183, Plate 68-design 201-202) or to fill in empty space (Plate 56-design 185).

Almost all of the designs have a mirror symmetry. On the symmetry line there is a candelabra, a vase or a similar type of object.

There is a group of designs with no motifs at all. It is as if the decorative border has become the main theme. The designs are in black with a few cross-stitches in red or a small medallion with a red background (Plate 84 and 85, designs 225-231).

Because it is counted embroidery, the stitches outlining the motifs are made horizontally, vertically or diagonally at an angle under 45 degrees. In a few designs no diagonal stitches are used (Plate 57-design 186, Plate 59-design 191). There are also a few designs in which just one or two diagonal stitches are used (Plate 58-design 189, Plate 61-design 193).

Execution of design 176 on plate 48. The running stitches all are made horizontally or vertically, with the exception of two diagonally made stitches

All of these designs look more primitive. According to Chiara Cernetti Batistelli, the source of these designs is from the thirteenth and fourteenth centuries. This source must have been filet lace. Filet lace is made by first making a net. The design is achieved by filling in some squares of the net and leaving other squares open. There are no diagonal lines. It is known that this kind of lace was made all over Italy during the fourteenth century. Unfortunately, I have never seen a piece of fourteenth century filet lace that I could directly link to the designs of Chiara Cernetti Batistelli.

Execution of design 182, plate 53 by Jos Hendriks

Execution of design 208, plate 74 by Jos Hendriks

Some information about the designs

Below is some information about every design in this book.
The enumeration on all plates is from left to right and up to down. The number of designs on each plate is indicated and a bit of information is included about the form of the design (square, circular, with repetition, etc.). After the general information for each plate there is information about each design on that plate.

The information about each design starts with a description or sometimes with a name. This description is usually a comment about the main motif. After the description between the 'and ', there is an abbreviation that indicates the origin of the design. The abbreviations are as follows:

    DMC (Dolfuss-Mieg Company)
    ANC (Ancora)
    C.C.B (Chiara Cernetti Battisti)
    L.V(L. Vannini)
    E.M.L(Eva Maria Leszner)
    R.B.C (Raffaella Bartolucci Cesaretti)
    J.H. (Jos Hendriks)

For a detailed explanation of these abbreviations, see the end of this chapter. If there is only a question mark then I don't remember where I found the design. Finally, the size of the design is given as the number of stitches horizontally times the number of stitches vertically (24x27, for example). If here is a repeating motif, the size of just that single motif is indicated.

Plate 1 Nine small, simple borders with repetitive design
'Duck', DMC and J.H., motif 7x11
'Bird', DMC and J.H., motif 9x12
'Birds', DMC and J.H., motif 14x15
'Birds', ?, motif 24x13
'Birds', ?, motif 22x23
'Birds', ?, motif 30x20
'Bird and flower', C.C.B., decorative border J.H., 24x27
'Duck's C.C.B., 44x34
'Birds', L.V., motif 35x22

Plate 2 Seven small borders with medallion and repeating pattern
'Duck' DMC, motif 20x12
'Birds', C.C.B., motif 40x35
'Duck', DMC, motif 28x30
'Duck', DMC, motif 44x24
'Bird', C.C.B., and J.H., motif 32x25
'Goose', ?, motif 31x21
'Bird', C.C.B., motif 60x43

Plate 3 Six small borders with repeating pattern
'Ducks', DMC, motif 40x31
'Birds', DMC, motif 31x35
'Birds, ?, motif 50x41

'Birds', C.C.B., motif 21x20
'Birds', DMC, motif 42x17
'Birds', DMC, motif 44x29

Plate 4 Five borders with repeating pattern
'Birds', C.C.B., decorative border J.H., 48x46
'Birds', C.C.B., motif 44x34
'Birds', DMC, motif 36x31
'Birds DMC, motif 35x47
'Ducks', DMC, motif 44x34

Plate 5 Four borders with repetition
'Bird', ANC, motif 42x52
'Eagle and other birds', ANC., motif 36x41
'Birds', DMC, motif 44x38
'Swans', DMC, motif 82x57

Plate 6 Four borders with repetition
'Deer', C.C.B., motif 52x30
'Dogs', DMC, motif 39x49
'Dogs', R.B.C, motif 62x36
'Hares', C.C.B., motif 56x48

Plate 7 Medallion, two borders with repetition and a squared border, all with the same bird motif
'Two birds', DMC, 45x32
'Scroll work with medallion with one bird', DMC and J.H., motif 40x28
'Medallions with two birds in square border', DMC and J.H., 117x117
'Same as before but the bird is looking in the other direction', DMC and J.H., motif 40x28

Plate 8 Two small squared borders and one rectangular border
'Little birds', ?, 61x61
'Medallions with ducks in scroll work', E.M.L., 70x70
'Birds', ANC, adapted to a square J.H., 145x109

Plate 9 One small rectangular border
'Leaves', J.H from traditional motif, 150x118, free inner space 82x50

Plate 10 One squared border and one border with medallions
'Bird', ANC, decorative border J.H., 138x138, free inner space 34x34
'Doggies', A.B., motif 65x37

Plate 11 Four borders with repetition
'Birds', C.C.B., decorative border J.H., motif 43x35
'Birds', C.C.B., decorative border J.H., motif 33x50
'Birds', C.C.B., decorative border J.H., motif 55x40
'Birds', C.C.B., decorative border J.H., motif 35x46

Plate 12 Four borders with repetition
'Birds', C.C.B., motif 56x42
.'Birds', C.C.B., motif 46x49
.'Birds', C.C.B., decorative border J.H., motif 46x38

'Birds', C.C.B., motif 52x42

Plate 13 Two borders with repetition, two small squares, one medallion
'Bird couple', C.C.B., motif 134x58
'Drinking birds', C.C.B., contour border J.H., 59x59 or 59x71
'Birds at drinking place', C.C.B., 30x26
'Birds feeding their young', ANC, 51x50
'Birds around drinking bowl', C.C.B., motif 60x72

Plate 14 Twelve small medallions
'Two birds', C.C.B., 35x48
'Bird', C.B.B., 43x43
'Bird on a branch', DMC, 44x44
'Two birds', C.C.B., 33x33
'Dragon', C.C.B., 55x55
'Eagle', ANC, 27x27
'Birds', DMC, 29x39
'Birds', C.C.B., 74x74
'Flying bird', ?, 40x40
'Bird', C.C.B., 23x23
'Bird', C .C.B., 27x27
'Bird', C.C.B., 26x26

Plate 15 Twelve small medallions
.'Bird looking to the right', C.C.B., 62x60
.'Bird looking to the left', C.C.B., 62x60
.'Dragon', C.C.B., decorative border J.H., 108x100
'4 Small designs with lion, eagle, beast, horses', ANC, 31x31
'5 Small designs with flower motifs', ANC, 31x31

Plate 16 Three medallions
.'Swan', DMC, 80x56
.'Two birds', C.C.B., 105x105

Plate 17 Three medallions
'Two beasts, C.C.B., 124x134
'Beast looking to the right',C.C.B., 59x57
.'Beast looking to the left', C.C.B., 59x57

Plate 18 Three Medallions
'Two doves', C.C.B., 124x134
.'Dove looking to the left', C.C.B., 59x57
'Dove looking to the right', C.C.B., 59x57

Plate 19 Five designs, two rectangular, two nearly rectangular, one irregular

'Fantasy animals', C.C.B., 104x49
'Four fantasy animals, two mirrorplanes', J.H., 64x117
'Birds', R.B.C., 87x88
'Birds', R.B.C., 64x43

'Birds', R.B.C., 76x41

Plate 20 Three corner pieces and two irregular designs
.'Birds', R.B.C., 68x68
.'Fantasy animals', R.B.C., 80x80
.'Peacocks', R.B.C., 147x93
'Birds', R.B.C., 57x65
'Beasts', R.B.C., 103x103

Plate 21 One small rectangular design and six medallions
'Faces and birds', C.C.B., 111x34
'Animals', ANC, 47x48
'Beasts and Branches', ANC, 48x49
'Griffon', ANC, 53x53
'Bird', ANC, 47x47
'Bird', ANC, 47x47
'Birds', ANC, 50x50

Plate 22 One square, one circular and two irregular designs
'Birds and plant motifs', ANC, 87x87
'Double medallion with birds', ANC, 73x43
'Double medallion', C.C.B., 58x31
'Medallion with panthers', J.H., 49x50

Plate 23 Two borders and a small circular design and two small square designs
'Stylized plant motifs', ANC., motif 78x83
'Plant motifs and scroll work', E.M.L. and J.H., motif 49x55
'Circle with plant motifs', E.M.L, 63x63
'Small scroll work square', J.H., 42x42
'Scroll work square', E.M.L., 61x61

Plate 24 Four designs with repetition
'Birds', C.C.B., motif 45x29
'Birds', C.C.B., decorative border J.H., motif 55x47
'Birds', C.C.B., motif 70x52
'Birds', C.C.B., decorative border J.H., motif 66x48

Plate 25 One rectangular design
'Bird-tree', C.C.B., composition and decorative border J.H., 61x156, possible rectangles 61x(72+Nx28)

Plate 26 Three borders with repetition
'Fantasy animals', C.C.B., motif 57x99
'Fantasy animals', C.C.B., motif 158x51
'Fantasy animals', C.C.B., decorative border J.H., motif 86x45

'Plate 27 Three borders with repetition
'Dancing deer', C.C.B., motif 99x92
'Deer', C.C.B., decorative border J.H., motif 84x37
'Dancing deer', C.C.B., motif 66x56

Plate 28 Three borders with repetition
 'Winged beasts', ANC., motif 98x43
 'Onagers', C.C.B., decorative border J.H., motif 68x53
 'Fantasy animals', ?, motif 96x109

Plate 29 Two borders with repetition
 'Panthers', ?, motif 90x82
 'Birds', ?, motif 147x118

Plate 30 Three borders with repetition
 'Lions with scepter and ball', C.C.B., decorative border J.H., motif 139x60
 'Fantasy beasts', J.H., with traditional motifs, motif 90x60
 'Dragons', DMC, motif 93x68

Plate 31 Five borders with repetition
 'Fantasy animals', ANC, motif 67x38
 .'Leaves', ANC, decorative border J.H., motif 50x38
 .'Roosters', ANC, decorative border J.H., motif 76x35
 .'Swans', ANC, motif 98x35
 .'Hares', C.C.B., motif 56x40

Plate 32 Three borders with repetition
 .'Roosters', C.C.B., decorative border J.H., motif 72x59
 .'Winged beasts', DMC, motif 74x75
 .'Owls, Vultures, Foxes', ANC, border J.H., motif 92x65

Plate 33 Three borders with repetition
 'Peacocks', C.C.B., decorative border J.H., motif 82x51
 .'Swans', C.C.B., decorative border J.H., motif 64x71
 .'Roosters', C.C.B., decorative border J.H., motif155x86

Plate 34 Four borders with repetition
 .'Little beasts', DMC, motif 39x49
 .'Birds', ANC, decorative border J.H., motif 36x41
 .'Fantasy animal', C.C.B., decorative border J.H., motif 61x56
 'Little winged beasts', C.C.B., motif 81x66

Plate 35 Three borders with repetition
 'Victorian I', J.H., 110x61
 'Victorian II', J.H., 184x41
 'Victorian III', J.H., 120x81

Plate 36 Three borders with repetition
 'Lions', ?, motif 46x104
 'Seahorses', B.B.C., border J.H, motif 135x120
 'Birds', ?, 69x39

Plate 37 Border square
 'Birds and branches', DMC, 222x222, free inner space 86x86

Plate 38 One square
'Fantasy animals', DMC, centre J.H., 177x177

Plate 39 One border square
'Dragons', DMC with corner and adaptation to a square J.H., 178x178, free inner space 42x42

Plate 40 Border square
'Square with swans and in the corners a tree with birds', E.M.L., adaptations for square J.H, 78x178, free inner space 42x42

Plate 41 One rectangular design and a corner piece
'Swans with a tree with birds in the corners', E.M.L., adaptation for square J. H., 261x261, possible rectangles (194+N x 67) x (194+M x 67)
'Corner piece with swans and a tree with birds', E.M.L., 102x102

Plate 42 Border square and border with repetition
'Scroll work border with 4 medallions with small sea horses', ?, 197x197, free inner space 39x139
'Sea horses', C.C.B., motif 56x47

Plate 43 One border square
'Square from scroll work and corner pieces with seahorses', ?, some adaptations J.H, 378x378

Plate 44 Two borders with repetition
'Beasts and plants', C.C.B., one side worked open, motif 113x81
'Bird and beast around vase', C.C.B., decorative border J.H., motif 189x89

Plate 45 Two borders with repetition
'Horses', C.C.B., decorative border J.H., motif 118x117
'Donkeys', C.C.B., motif 114x112

Plate 46 Two borders with repetition
'Fantasy beasts', C.B.B., decorative border J.H., motif 154x124
'Winged horses', DMC, motif 118x85

Plate 47 Three borders with repetition
'Lions and griffons in a row', C.B.B., decorative border J.H., motif 110x90
'Dancing animals', ?, motif 94x67
'Fantasy beasts', DMC, motif 130x66

Plate 48 One border with repetition, one border square
'Eagles', ANC, decorative border J.H., motif 110x47
'Fantasy beasts', DMC, 160x160, free inner space 57x57

Plate 49 One border with repetition
'Animals around medallion with an eagle', C.C.B., decorative border J.H., a third color is used for the medallion, motif 170x136

Plate 50 One border with repetition
'Fantasy animals', C.C.B., decorative border J.H., motif 155x155

Plate 51 One border with repetition
'Winged beasts, small birds', C.C.B., decorative border J.H., motif 138x127

Plate 52 One border
'Beast around vase', C.C.B., decorative border J.H., 210x121

Plate 53 One border
‚Shelled border composition', J.H. with traditional motifs, decorative border J.H., motif 93x140

Plate 54 One border with repetition
'Fantasy animals and birds', DMC, decorative border J.H., motif 129x136,

Plate 55 One border with repetition
'Fantasy animals and birds', C.C.B., decorative border J.H., motif 180x183

Plate 56 Rectangular design
'Abundance', R.B.C., some corrections J.H., 232x160

Plate 57 Two borders with repetition
'Birds and tower', C.C.B., decorative border J.H., motif 101x91
'Birds', C.C.B., motif 96x112

Plate 58 Two borders with repetition
'Winged animals', C.C.B., decorative border J.H., motif 166x92
'Birds', C.C.B., decorative border J.H., motif 110x130

Plate 59 Two borders with repetition
'Fantasy animals', C.C.B. 160x88
'Birds', C.C.B., decorative border J.H., motif 85x110

Plate 60 One border with repetition
'Birds and snakes', C.C.B., decorative border J.H., 204x155

Plate 61 One border with repetition
'Falconer', C.C.B., decorative border J.H., motif 198x126

Plate 62 One border with repetition
'Dogs with balls', C.C.B., decorative border J.H., motif 160x141

Plate 63 One Border
'Grape-tails', DMC, 217x97

Plate 64 One border with repetition
'Fantasy animals', reconstruction from a photo, J.H., exactly one repetition is shown, the border with flower motifs is not in sync. with the main design, 263x114

Plate 65 One border with repetition
'Fantasy animals', DMC, motif 157x153

Plate 66 One border with repetition
'Exotic human-like figures', B.B.C., decorative border J.H., motif 152x198

Plate 67 Two borders with repetition
'Horn of abundance', J.H., motif 171x117
'Birds', C.C.B., decorative border J.H., motif 133x92

Plate 68 Square border design
'Large square border', R.B.C., 700x700, see also Plate 93

Plate 69 Circular design
'Shield', DMC, 165x165

Plate 70 Square
'Fantasy animals', DMC, 216x216

Plate 71 Square
'Fantasy animals', DMC, decorative border J.H., 204x204

Plate 72 Border square
'16 Beasts', DMC, 200x200, inner free space 48x48

Plate 73 Square
'Corner pieces with winged beasts', J.H. from a photograph of a traditional corner piece, 198x198

Plate 74 Square
'Mermen', DMC, decorative border J.H., 226x226

Plate 75 One rectangular design and one border with repetition
'Fantasy animals', J.H., 127x130
'Fantasy animals', C.C.B., motif 136x90

Plate 76 Two rectangular border designs
'Scroll work with two filled rectangles on the short side', L.V., 186x123, inner free space 86x97
'Scroll work with two filled rectangles on the short side', L.V., 178x100, inner free space 68x50

Plate 77 Four designs, one border square, one square and two borders
'Border square with shelled edge inside', L.V., 170x170
'Almost square with two beasts', L.V., 52x46
'Border with square medallions', L.V., motif 29x17
'Border with square medallions', L.V., motif 29x17

Plate 78 Border square
'Fantasy birds', ?, 215x215

Plate 79 Border square
'Sea life', J.H. with motifs from C.C.B., 345x345, inner free space 109x109

Pate 80 Border square
'Birds', DMC, 181x181, inner free space 77x77

Plate 81 Border square
'Fantasy animals and birds', DMC, 314x314, inner free space 162x162

Plate 82 Border square
'Square with shelled edge and with lions and swans', R.B.C., 330x330, inner free space 208x208

Plate 83 Three scroll work with medallion designs
'Square with birds',, E.M.L 117x117
'Square with flowers', J.H., 50x50
'Irregular design with birds and flowers', J.H., 100x41

Plate 83 Three scroll work with medallion designs
'Square with birds', E.M.L., 117x117
'Square with flowers', J.H., 50x50
'Irregular design with birds and flowers', J.H., 100x41

Plate 84 Two scroll work designs
'Plain filling', E.M.L. and J.H., eight different building blocks 26x26
'A square', E.M.L., 124x124

Plate 85 Five scroll work designs
'Square', J.H., 88x88
'Square', J.H., 56x56
'Square', J.H., 66x66
'Square', J.H., 51x51
'Square', J.H., 49x49

Plate 86 Two scroll work designs
'Five squares in a square', E.M.L., 148x148
'Art Deco', C.C.B. and J.H., motif: 78x47

Plate 87 Oval design without a decorative edge
'Several birds around a vase', ?, there is a horizontal and a vertical mirror line, 245x175

Plate 88 One square with scroll work, 2 scroll work borders and one rectangular design.
'Scroll work square', J.H., 73x73
'Scroll work border', J.H., motif 19x19
'Scroll work border', J.H., motif 21x21
'Celtic dragon', J.H., 169x87

Plate 89 Circular design
'Fantasy animals', R.B.C., 153x155

Plate 90 One rectangular border and one border with repetition.
'Fantasy animals', J.H., 109x134
'Fantastic animals', DMC, 96x86

Plate 91 Rectangular design
'Unicorns', J.H., 208x160

Plate 92 Border with repetition
'Winged lion and head', J.H., motif 427x127

Plate 93 Border square with 5 medallions inside
'Masterpiece', Border itself R.B.C., central medallion DMC, other medallions: R.B.C., but rotated 45 degrees by J.H., 700x700.

Explanation of the abbreviations used

DMC: Dolfuss-Mieg and Company,
A French company that produced yarn and published many pattern books, one of which was "Assisi Embroidery". It has been published in French, English, German and Italian, presumably in the 1950s. Some of the designs in this book I also found in older publications. It is not clear whether there are also original designs.

ANC: Ancora, an Italian company that produced yarn. They also edited a book with Assisi patterns in the 1950s. The title is "Punto Assisi and Punto Scritto".

CCB: Chiara Cernetti Battistelli is the author of the pattern book "Punto Assisi" which was published in Italian and French in 1926.
This was my most important source. It has a very large collection of original designs, many of which you can also find in later publications.

L.V: L. Vannini is the author of the two oldest pattern booklets I know of. They were published under the name of Lavoro Assisiano 1 and 2. There are only original patterns.

E.M.L: Eva Maria Leszner, author of a pattern book (English edition 1988) with clear designs that aren't too big. Many of these designs I also found in older publications. Patterns like those on Plates 83, 84 and 85 I could not find anywhere else.

RBC: Raffaella Bartolucci Cesaretti. Her book "Il Punto Assisi" is mainly about the history of the style. At the end of the book there are some beautiful patterns. A few of the designs in this book are reconstructions made with the help of a photograph from that book. (Plate 64, design 196).

A.B: Alida Becchetti. "Punto Assisi", published by Minerva, 1999

Execution of design 197, plate 65 by Jos Hendriks

Execution of design 135, plate 30 by Jos Hendriks

The designs

Plate 1

designs 1-9

Plate 2

designs 10-16

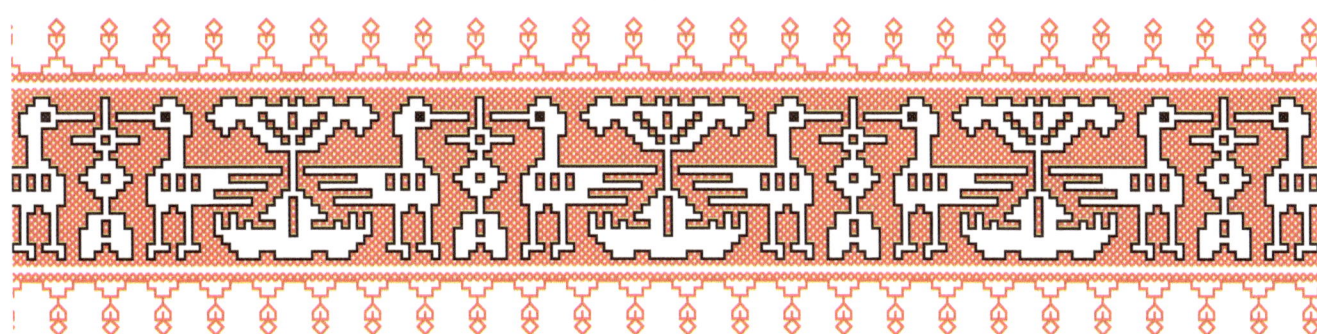
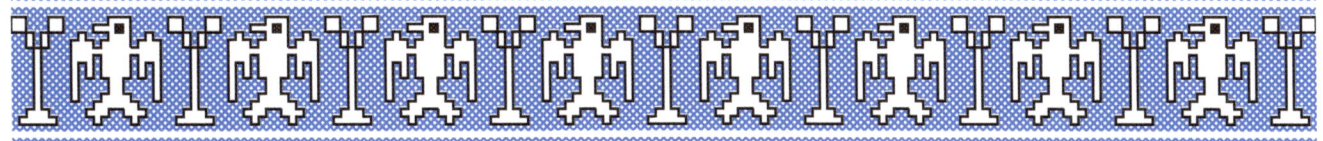

Plate 3

designs 17-22

Plate 4

designs 23-27

Plate 5

designs 28-31

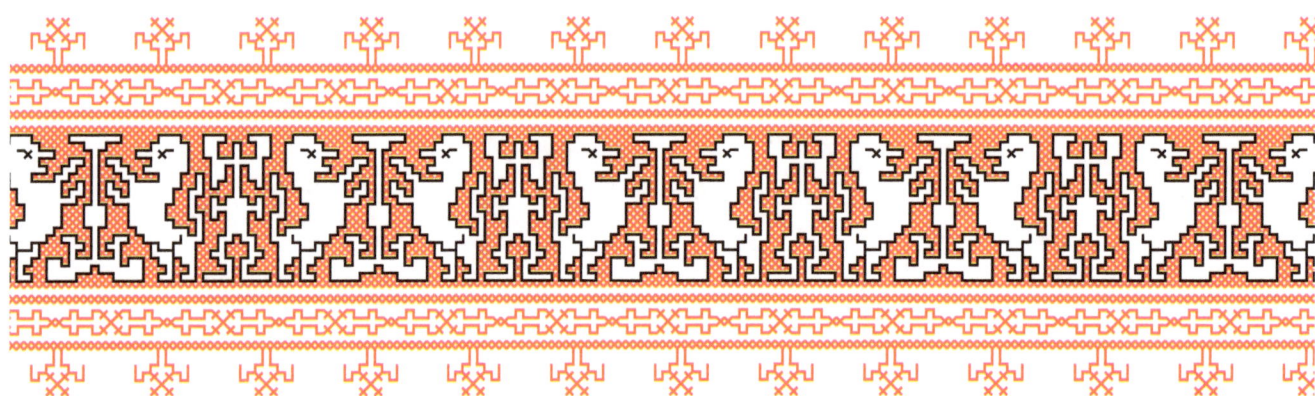

Plate 6

designs 32-35

Plate 7

designs 36-39

Plate 8

designs 40-42

Plate 9

design 43

Plate 10

designs 44-45

Plate 11

designs 46-49

Plate 12

designs 50-53

Plate 13

designs 54-58

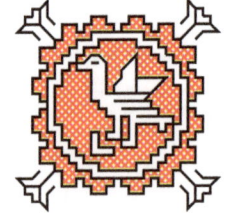

Plate 14

designs 59-70

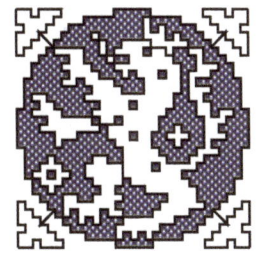   
 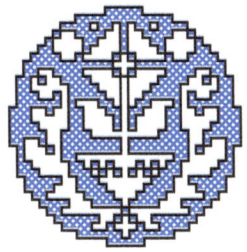  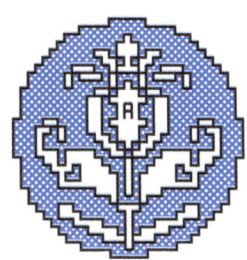 

Plate 15

designs 71-82

Plate 16

designs 83-85

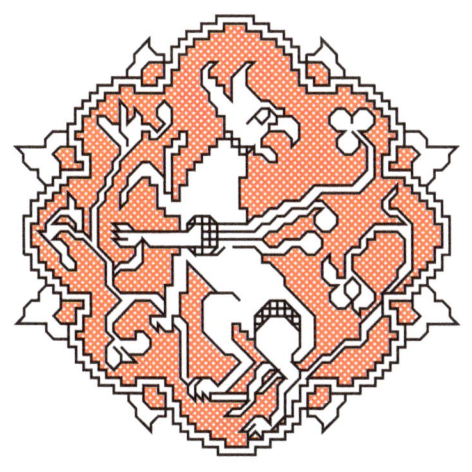

Plate 17

designs 86-88

Plate 18

designs 89-91

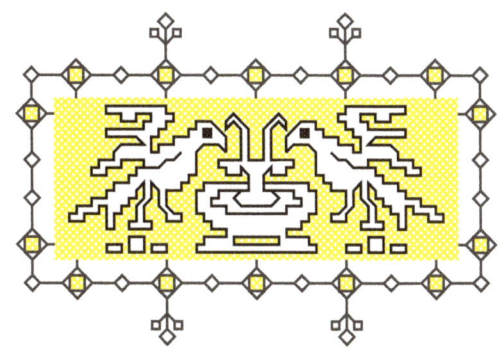

Plate 19

designs 92-96

Plate 20

designs 97-101

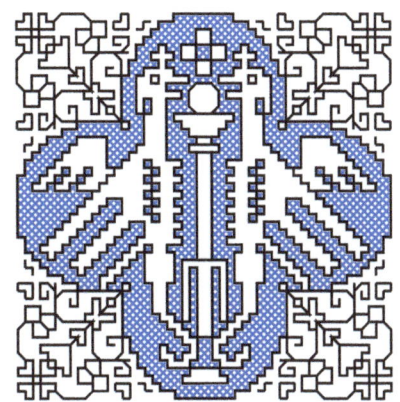

Plate 21

designs 102-108

Plate 22

designs 109-112

Plate 23

designs 113-117

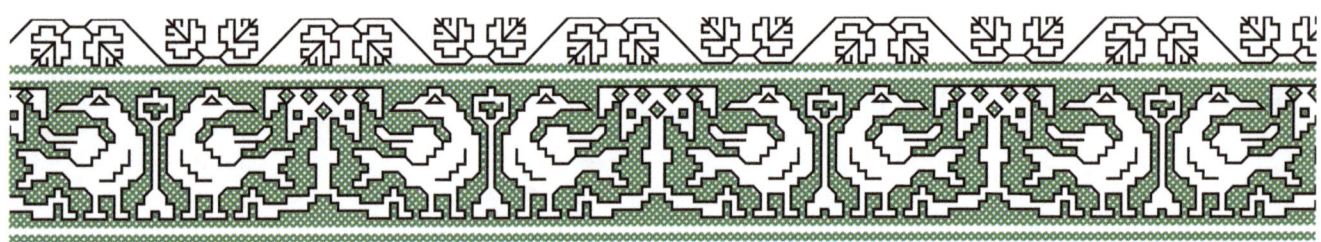

Plate 24

designs 118-121

Plate 25

design 122

Plate 26

designs 123-125

Plate 27

designs 126-128

Plate 28

designs 129-131

Plate 29

designs 132-133

Plate 30

designs 134-136

Plate 31

designs 137-141

Plate 32

designs 142-144

Plate 33

designs 145-147

Plate 34

designs 148-151

Plate 35

designs 152-154

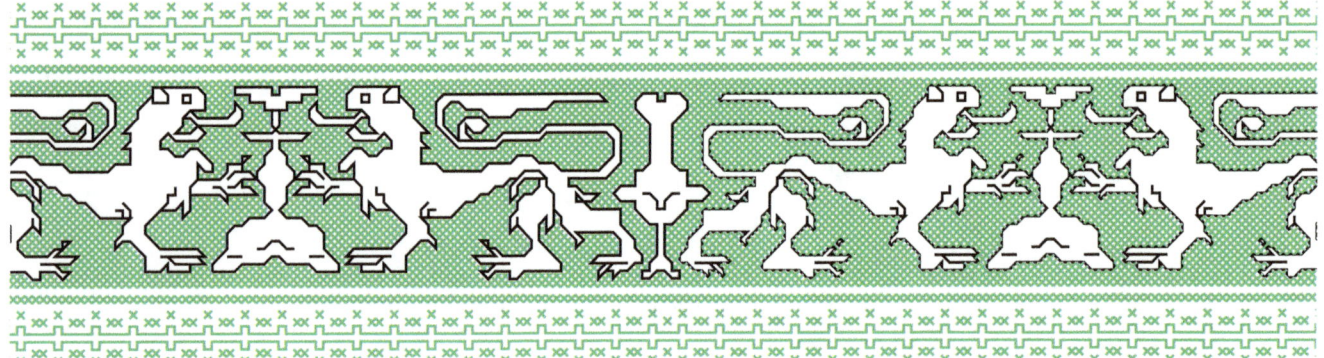

Plate 36

designs 155-157

Plate 37

design 158

Plate 38

design 159

Plate 39

design 160

Plate 40

design 161

Plate 41

designs 162-163

Plate 42

designs 164-165

Plate 43

design 166

Plate 44

designs 167-168

Plate 45

designs 169-170

Plate 46

designs 171-172

Plate 47

designs 173-175

Plate 48

designs 176-177

Plate 49

design 178

Plate 50

design 179

Plate 51

design 180

Plate 52

design 181

Plate 53

design 182

Plate 54

design 183

Plate 55

design 184

Plate 56

design 185

Plate 57

designs 186-187

Plate 58

designs 188-189

Plate 59

designs 190-191

Plate 60

design 192

Plate 61

design 193

Plate 62

design 194

Plate 63

design 195

Plate 64

design 196

Plate 65

design 197

Plate 66

design 198

Plate 67

designs 199-200

Plate 68

designs 201-202

Plate 69

design 203

Plate 70

design 204

Plate 71

design 205

Plate 72

design 206

Plate 73

design 207

Plate 74

design 208

Plate 75

designs 209-210

Plate 76

designs 211-212

Plate 77

designs 213-216

Plate 78

design 217

Plate 79

design 218

Plate 80

design 219

Plate 81

design 220

Plate 82

design 221

Plate 83

designs 222-224

Plate 84

designs 225-226

Plate 85

designs 227–231

Plate 86

designs 232-233

Plate 87

design 234

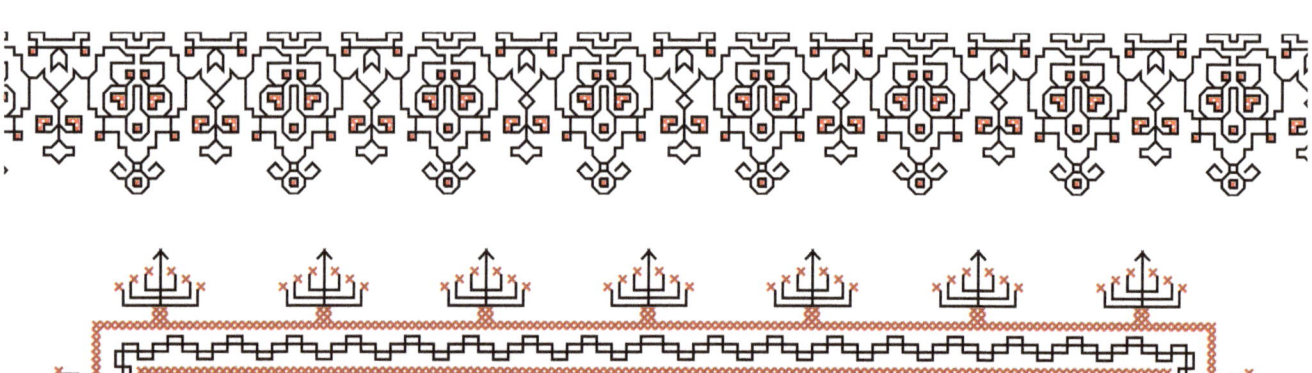

Plate 88

designs 235-238

Plate 90

designs 240-241

Plate 91

design 242

Plate 92

design 243

Plate 93

design 244

www.ingramcontent.com/pod-product-compliance
Lightning Source LLC
Chambersburg PA
CBHW061353010526
44107CB00011B/927